Faith ar

Close Encounters of an Evangelistic Kind

Ian Maher

Tutor and Lecturer,

Wilson Carlile College of Evangelism, Sheffield

Church Army Evangelist

GROVE BOOKS LIMITED

RIDLEY HALL RD CAMBRIDGE CB3 9HU

Contents

Acknowledgment
With thanks to my research assistant, Ms A S Peck

The Cover Illustration is by Peter Ashton

First Impression August 2002
ISSN 1367-0840
ISBN 1 85174 507 6

Introduction

'I guess I could be pretty pissed off about what happened to me...but it's hard to stay mad when there's so much beauty in the world. Sometimes I feel like I'm seeing it all at once, and it's too much, my heart fills up like a balloon that's about to burst...and then I remember to relax, and stop trying to hold on to it, and then it flows through me like rain and I can't feel anything but gratitude for every single moment of my stupid little life...You have no idea what I'm talking about, I'm sure. But don't worry...You will someday.'

Lester Burnham[1]

Those words drew the Oscar-winning film *American Beauty* to a close. In a voice-over, the main character of the film is reflecting on life from the perspective of his untimely death. His comments effectively draw together the threads of a story about a dysfunctional middle-class American suburban family and imbue them with a sense of transcendence. *American Beauty* could not be described as an overtly religious film, yet it resonates with deep questions about the human condition: Who am I? Why am I here? Where am I going?

Such questions are often not far from the surface of many popular films, making it important for the churches to develop an ongoing dialogue with film. Film is now 'the medium of the masses,' facing the churches with both a challenge and an evangelistic opportunity.[2] The challenge is to engage with the medium, recognizing the deep currents that film stirs in the hearts and minds of those who watch. The evangelistic opportunity is to bring the good news of Jesus Christ into conversation with a widely shared expression of popular culture.

Film is now the 'medium of the masses,' facing the churches with both a challenge and an evangelistic opportunity

For some this may seem a dubious venture. There are those who would see little scope for engagement with the standard 'secular' fare of the multiplexes, fearing that their faith will be tarnished by such worldliness. Others will be distanced by what they regard as a specialist area of ministry, requiring the acquisition of considerable film critical knowledge and technical know-how. On each count, the reasons for opting out are unfounded. Such perceived obstacles should not prevent anyone with an interest in connecting the gospel with contemporary culture from having a go. All that is needed is an enthusiasm for film, a passion for the gospel, and maybe a little help to get started.

My hope is that if you already use film in your ministry you will be encouraged by this booklet. If it represents a new venture, I hope it will give you the confidence to join the growing number of people who are excited by film's potential for opening up discussion about the things that matter most in the journey through life. Chapters 2 and 3 set the scene by providing a theoretical base for an evangelistic encounter between faith and film. Chapters 4 and 5 reflect on practice and offer and some tried and tested approaches plus details of some useful resources.

2   The Impact of Film Upon Contemporary Culture

'I meet people occasionally who think motion pictures, the product Hollywood makes, is merely entertainment, has nothing to do with education. That's one of the darndest fool fallacies that is current...Anything that brings you to tears by way of drama does something to the deepest roots of our personality. All movies, good or bad, are educational and Hollywood is the foremost educational institution on earth. What, Hollywood more important than Harvard? The answer is not as clean as Harvard, but nevertheless farther reaching.'

Carl Sandberg, former US poet laureate[3]

People watch films, and they watch lots of them, whether on television, on video, or at the cinema. In fact cinema attendance is booming despite a series of predictions that it was doomed.[4]

In the context of film-watching at the cinema, there is something about being together in a darkened auditorium and dwarfed by the images projected on a screen that has a fascination and attraction about it. And whether it is the power of the film, the shared experience, or both that triggers a response in people, the fact that there *is* a response is indisputable. This becomes apparent to anyone leaving a cinema after a film through listening to and watching the words and responses of the viewers. Sometimes people leave in silence, sometimes in laughter. There might be anger or sadness. Films connect with the whole range of human emotions, sometimes working away well beyond the occasion on which a film is viewed.

Films can also span the generations in a way that books are less able to do in a culture that communicates increasingly through visual media. Christians cannot afford to be *out of touch* with popular film if they are to remain *in touch* with the swirling currents of contemporary society.

The Fascination of Film

In an age of sound-bite communication in which we are told that realistic attention spans are approximately twenty minutes long, film confounds conventional wisdom. Consider an auditorium of several hundred people gathered together to view a two-hour film. With few exceptions, those present have little problem in remaining focused on the film. There is also far less fidgeting than is often apparent during a twenty-minute Sunday sermon! Similarly, many people have little trouble in settling down in front of the TV to watch a feature film. So what is the fascination inherent in film?

Perhaps it is because films tell stories. Although a relatively new art form (a little over a century old) film is simply a new angle on an ancient convention. In every culture, customs and traditions have been transmitted across the generations through storytelling. Film is the development of tales told around the camp fire and in the pages of literature. It has the same power to touch hearts and minds.

A story to challenge King David's adultery had more chance of hitting the mark than a lecture about morality

Ken Gire effectively uses the example of the story told by the prophet Nathan to King David in making this point.[5] Nathan knew that a story to challenge King David's adultery with Bathsheba had more chance of hitting the mark than a lecture about morality. Stories have the capacity to slip under our guard and when they do, something extraordinary happens. 'We feel something. We may feel outrage, as David did, or any number of other emotions—fear, guilt, shame, empathy, compassion, joy, sorrow, love, hate.'[6]

Those who dismiss film as nothing more than entertainment (as if entertainment is, in itself, of little value) would do well to ponder T S Eliot's reflection on literature, words which equally apply to the work of a film director:

'The author of a work of imagination is trying to affect us wholly, as human beings, whether he (*sic*) knows it or not; we are affected by it, as human beings, whether we intend to be or not.'[7]

Films affect us both at a conscious and an unconscious level. The extent will vary from superficial to profound, but there is often some degree of resonance with our own experience. That is why even the most ordinary of films can sometimes touch us in unexpected ways.[8] It also explains why the person sitting next to you in the cinema can be doubled up with laughter or overcome with grief at events in a film while you remain unmoved, or *vice versa*.

Even the most ordinary of films can sometimes touch us in unexpected ways

Roger Angell writes: 'Going to the movies, in fact, is not an intellectual process most of the time but an emotional one. Any serious, well made movie we see seems to wash over us there in the dark, bathing us in feelings and suggestions, and imparting a deep or light tinge of meaning that stays with us, *sometimes for life*' (italics mine).[9] Though the comment refers to the encounter with film at the cinema, the same observations are relevant to films viewed on the small screen. The emotional impact of a film is experienced to a greater or lesser extent whether the viewer is consciously aware of it or not. All the more reason for Christians to develop the basic skills of teasing out the issues and implications that are raised. Some contend that film is becoming 'the most potent vehicle of teachers and parents for imparting the values of our heritage' and that they might one day become the primary texts of our society.[10]

The Pervasiveness of Film

Some striking film-watching figures emphasize the pervasiveness of film in contemporary society.[11]

- During the year 2000 cinema attendances alone in the UK topped 142 million—approaching three million per week.

- Over two million 7- to 14-year-olds, four million 15- to 24-year-olds, and three million 25- to 34-year-olds visited the cinema at least once a month.

- Between 1989 and 1999 the number of cinema screens rose by almost 1,200 to 2,758.

- Over the same period video retail transactions rose from 38 million to 96 million (plus four million DVDs in 1999).

Interestingly, there were well over seven million cinema attendances each month for people in the age category 15 to 34. The same age range is often absent in the churches, emphasizing the urgent need for Christians to take film seriously as a significant expression of popular culture.

The Impact of Film Upon Contemporary Culture

One of the hot debates concerning film is the extent to which it affects the values, attitudes and behaviour of those who watch them. While cause-and-effect arguments are difficult to sustain, there are plenty of indicators concerning the influential nature of film.

Merchandising and Marketing

Films such as *Lord of the Rings: The Fellowship of the Ring* (Peter Jackson, 2001), *Harry Potter and the Philosopher's Stone* (Chris Columbus, 2001), *Spiderman* (Sam Raimi, 2002) and *Star Wars Episode II: Attack of the Clones* (George Lucas, 2002), have a vast range of accompanying themed goods including toys, books, T-shirts, game cards, and computer games. The revenues generated are huge. It has been estimated that the total gross income for the first 'Harry Potter' film, including all the associated merchandising, could reach a staggering *$1 billion*. In any event, the film broke opening weekend box-office records on both sides of the Atlantic as cinemas were besieged by 'muggles'[12] intent on seeing their hero.

There is a clear line of logic at work in film marketing and merchandising

In addition to themed merchandising, films provide lucrative advertising opportunities through the concept of product placement. Characters will be wearing designer label products, driving a particular type of vehicle, drinking a certain brand of beer, or using a specific mobile phone. In each case, at some point in the film the name of the manufacturer of the product is clearly made evident. It can be assumed that the choices of the viewing public are influenced by this.

There is a clear line of logic at work in relation to film marketing and merchandising and the potential of film to influence contemporary society. In a nutshell, successful advertising persuades people to buy the products in question. The placement of products in films and/or the linking of merchandise with films are part of a marketing strategy to promote sales of those products. If, therefore, films can contribute to people making decisions about how to spend their hard-earned money then there is an established link between what people see and how they behave. It is not as simple as cause-and-effect but there is a connection. The issue becomes more complex in relation to the film and violence debate.

The link between what people see and how they behave is not as simple as cause-and-effect, but there is a connection

The Portrayal of Violence in Film

A well-worn accusation levelled at the film industry is that its portrayal of violence is a major cause of violence in society. The accusations are understandable but are knee-jerk responses to sensational and extreme events picked up in the media.

- In the Jamie Bulger case (1993), following the arrest of children responsible for Jamie's brutal murder, the tabloid media pronounced that access to an adult-rated 'video nasty' was the cause of the boys' appalling actions.

- In 1998, a senior British policeman voiced his opinion that Hollywood was responsible for the rise of murders by 'hit-men.'[13]

- Following the fatal shooting of 15 people in a Colorado school during 1999, connections were made between the teenage killers who carried out the crime and *The Matrix* (Larry and Andy Wachowski, 1999). Such supposed links were voiced not only in the Press, but also by President Bill Clinton.[14]

- In April 2000 the British Press carried a report of a murder in Paris by a teenager dressed in the cape and mask that had become the hallmark of the *Scream* (Wes Craven, 1996) horror film franchise.

While the common sense arguments sound compelling, the evidence is less clear. A 1997 Home Office study challenged previous research suggesting links between screen violence and violent behaviour.[15] The report maintained that young people who do not experience violence in the family or have a criminal history will almost certainly *not* be moved to aggressive behaviour by violent films: 'The implication is that both a history of family violence and offending behaviour are necessary preconditions for developing a significant preference for violent film action and role models.'[16] Almost no evidence was found to suggest that film violence led directly to further aggression from any of the people studied. In summary, the findings were that violent films do not provoke young people; violence does, the roots of which are to be found elsewhere. Film is more a mirror of a violent society rather than a root cause. If that is so, the problems of a violent society will not be addressed by even the most draconian censorship.

Film is more a mirror of a violent society rather than a root cause

However, even in the absence of empirical evidence, some nagging questions remain about the frequent and graphic portrayal of violence in film. If film as a marketing medium can influence people's spending habits, it is difficult to dismiss the *possibility* of violent films adversely affecting the behaviour of some people with an existing tendency towards violence.

Film and Social Values

Once again, a complicated dynamic is at work. Film reflects social values, but there is also evidence to suggest that they are imparted through film. Research by the University of Colorado's centre for mass media into the source of young people's religious values pointed strongly to film.[17] The themes with which they were connecting were often those at the heart of Christian faith but film is proving to be a more relevant means of engagement for young people than are the churches.

Film also communicates powerfully about relationships, often implicitly endorsing popular trends. For instance, the individualistic and often casual attitudes toward sex in films may be more a reflection than a cause of the direction in which society has moved. Nevertheless, the dominant current in popular film reinforces such attitudes, confusing boundaries between sex and love and offering unrealistic ideals.

Similarly, the power of Hollywood in the film world promotes the individualistic and materialistic focus of American society as an ideal. Particular assumptions are presented as normative with regard to how the world is/should be understood and interpreted. We need to bring a critical perspective to bear upon the assumptions that are transmitted through film if we are to avoid the danger of being swept along by the value systems that they carry.

Why Christians Should Not Opt Out

With film woven into the very fabric of our society, it is difficult to see how Christians can remain aloof. I am not suggesting that *every* Christian should watch films, or that an undiscriminating stance should be adopted. Individual sensitivities vary and discernment is needed. But so, too, is a critical Christian perspective on the issues and themes of popular film. Surely it is better for the church to be involved in an ongoing dialogue with popular film, challenging where appropriate, rather than condemning from the sidelines? Uninformed, and sometimes unfounded, objections to particular films serve only to widen the credibility gap between Christians and the majority of people in contemporary society.

Uninformed, and sometimes unfounded, objections to particular films serve only to widen the credibility gap

In 1973 *The Exorcist* (William Friedkin) drew strong criticism from conservative Christian groups. Cinemas were picketed by Christians who had not seen the film. Some scenes *were* shocking and remain so even today. But the irony is that both the author[18] and the director of *The Exorcist* were Roman Catholics seeking to open people's eyes to the reality of God by highlighting the awful nature of evil that distorts God's creation. A considerable opportunity was missed by the churches to offer some informed response to the film. It touched a spiritual nerve in society and opened up a way for Christians to make links with the issues raised and the reality of a God who made the ultimate sacrifice to ensure the defeat of evil. Sadly, the rhetoric against the film prevented serious conversation from taking place.

More recently, *Dogma* (Kevin Smith, 1999) was criticized for being blasphemous. Irreverent it certainly is, but the film is actually God-affirming in an off-beat way. The film's barb lies in its ruthless attack on institutional religion. Again it was a missed opportunity, on this occasion to explore the difference between the substance and the packaging of religious faith in a society that is increasingly turning its back on institutional religion.

God may well be speaking into contemporary culture through the medium of film if only we have eyes to see and ears to hear

Such films are not for the easily offended, but it is important that *some* Christians engage with the standard fare of the multiplexes and the video shops, including the films that court controversy. That does not mean busy people needing to become professional film critics but simply that Christians who are already keen film-watchers consciously bring their faith perspective to bear on the issues raised.

Whether a film is supportive, subversive or antagonistic towards Christian values is secondary to the ability of the churches to make reasoned and relevant responses. A cultural phenomenon as huge as film should not be left unexamined. God may well be speaking into contemporary culture through the medium of film if only we have eyes to see and ears to hear.[19] Film has the capacity to surprise and challenge us, to disturb and provoke us, and to shake us out of our complacency. Sometimes it will cause us to take stock and consider how we might reinterpret and reapply our faith in ways that are relevant to the society and time in which we live.

Making Connections 3

'When I was a little younger...I wanted to be a priest. However, I soon realized that my real vocation, my real calling, was the movies. I don't really see a conflict between the church and the movies, the sacred and the profane. Obviously there are major differences. But I can also see great similarities between a church and a moviehouse. Both are places for people to come together and share a common experience. And I believe there's a spirituality in films, even if it's not one which can supplant faith...It's as if movies answer an ancient quest for the common unconscious. They fulfil a spiritual need that people have: to share a common memory.'

Martin Scorsese, film director[20]

The Spiritual Dimension of Film

Film can stir the human spirit. Through our identification with characters, stories, and situations portrayed in film, resonances are set up with our own spiritual yearning. Sometimes this transcends words and can only be described as an experiential encounter. Ken Gire captures this succinctly when he speaks of film drawing people 'with the hope of touching that divine garment we call life, not to analyse the weave or pick the lint off the garment.'[21] The interaction between faith and film is more about a dynamic encounter than a critical analysis of fine detail. It is about identifying those points of similarity and difference, comfort and challenge, harmony and dissonance that exist between the film story and the faith story of the viewer. This emphasis on encounter preserves the integrity of film and acknowledges its potential to affect a person's spiritual life.

> *The interaction between faith and film is more about a dynamic encounter than a critical analysis of fine detail*

Some words of C S Lewis about art also have relevance to film: 'We sit down before the picture in order to have something done to us, not that we might do things with it. The first demand that any work of art makes on you is surrender.'[22] Of course, not every film could be described as a work of art any more than every painting qualifies as a masterpiece. However, film *is* an art form and as such has the capacity to help us touch the transcendent. In the same way that a picture, a sculpture or a poem can convey something that goes beyond the paint, the clay, or the words from which they are created, film also can be more than the sum of its director, actors, cinematography and other constituents. That is a key reason why bells are rung at a spiritual level even when the subject matter has no overt religious content.

For a real encounter between faith and film to take place three steps are necessary: *experience, reflection* and *dialogue*. Firstly, a film must be *experienced* in its own right and be allowed to speak for itself. This means letting go of any preconceptions and allowing the film the chance to wash over us and engage us at every level. This would be a little scary and potentially quite dangerous were it not for the second step. *Reflection* on a film allows us to monitor our responses, acknowledging the thoughts, feelings and emotions evoked. From that considered position it becomes possible to bring personal faith perspectives and issues raised by the film into a constructive *dialogue*.

There will be occasions when a film triggers a real sense of epiphany in the viewer

The end result can vary. Sometimes the values and ideals carried within a film will conflict with the viewer's beliefs. At other times a sense of consistency will emerge even though faith and film might use different languages to articulate common perspectives. There will be occasions when a film triggers a real sense of epiphany in the viewer. For complex reasons involving the life experience of the viewer and a combination of factors within the film a fresh insight occurs and faith become enriched through the encounter.

Film as a Vehicle for Exploring Life's Big Questions

Film can touch the depths of our being. At its best, film confronts us with sublime truth about being human. Robert McKee, exploring the power of story, speaks of film as 'a two-hour metaphor that says: Life is like this.'[23] We may agree or disagree with the 'metaphor,' but either way the big questions are set before us and face us with certain implications. If life *is* as portrayed in a film it confronts us with the challenge of *how* we should live.

The film itself might offer its own answers that endorse or contradict our own response to the challenge. In this way we are drawn into the film, whether through a conscious reaction or by means of an internal dialogue at the level of our emotions. Sometimes, the encounter will precipitate change in a person. The following true story provides a profound example.

An employee of a Swiss bank uncovered some old documentation that was deliberately set aside for shredding. Skimming through the papers he realized that they were the financial accounts of Jewish people placed at the bank prior to the outbreak of World War II. The employee managed to remove the documents from the bank and he went public with them. The eventual outcome was a $1.2 billion dollar settlement for the holocaust survivors and their beneficiaries. The result for the employee himself was a string of hate letters and death threats that forced him to seek asylum. Why did he take such bold action and put himself at considerable risk? He tells how several days earlier he had seen Steven Spielberg's film *Schindler's List* (1993) and of how the film gave him the courage to make his stand and bring about some sense of justice for the Jewish people.[24]

Schindler's List is, of course, an immensely powerful film. Audiences left cinema screenings in stunned silence having been touched at the very depth of their being by the story of one flawed man's struggle to do something in the face of genocide. Relatively few films stir such strong responses but *most* films connect in some way with the human condition and the big questions of life that confront us all. This presents the churches with an unparalleled opportunity to engage Christian faith with an immensely popular expression of contemporary culture. It is a real chance to make relevant points of contact with large numbers of people who might never otherwise hear about the good news of Jesus Christ.

Discerning Themes and Issues

Sometimes the subject matter of a film will raise quite obvious themes and issues. For example, *Saving Private Ryan* (Steven Spielberg, 1998) and *The Thin Red Line* (Terrence Malick, 1998) provide a graphic insight into the horrors of war. In a similar way *Trainspotting* (Danny Boyle, 1995) and *Traffic* (Steven Soderbergh, 2000) offer a harrowing look at the consequences of drug misuse and the effect of the narcotics trade. It is not difficult to imagine how conversation between Christian faith and such films might develop. Questions about justice and peace, despair and hope, human dignity and self-worth quickly surface. At times a little more work is needed but it is well worth the effort.

In getting to grips with a film for yourself, and especially if you are planning to use a film to engage people in an exploration of faith, it is important that you have identified some of the significant points. You will not always get them all as different people will see different things in a film, but the following steps are helpful to bear in mind.[25]

1. Write a one-paragraph synopsis of the film—use your own words, imagining that you want to tell someone what the film is about.[26]

2. List what you see as the main theme(s) and key issues—in other words, what are the broad brushstrokes and what are the sharp features of the film? For example, in *American Beauty* (Sam Mendes, 1999) the Burnham family have lost their sense of purpose and meaning. This is a main theme. Some consequences for the Burnhams include an unhealthy attachment to possessions, an adulterous relationship for Carolyn and a pot-smoking habit for Lester. These are key issues. Sometimes themes and issues blur together but that does not matter. Their identification is more important than their classification.

3. Identify ways in which your Christian perspective on life reacts and relates to the theme(s) and issues that you have uncovered in the film—jotting down a few thoughts.

Having gone through those three steps, you will be in a good position to facilitate others in an encounter with the film. That does not mean imposing a rigid agenda but being able to guide a response while remaining flexible enough to allow the film to speak for itself.

Film as an Indicator of Some of the Pressing Concerns of Society—Some Examples

There will always be films in the public domain that touch on the big questions of life. Also, with reasonable regularity there are clusters of films released fairly close to each other with similar themes. This sometimes highlights a particular concern of society that is current, or persistent. Overarching human concerns often emerge in popular film.

Fears For The Future
Not surprisingly at the turn of the millennium, films such as *Armageddon* (Michael Bay, 1998) and *Deep Impact* (Mimi Leder, 1998) appeared on the big screen. Both films depicted the scenario of earth being devastated by a meteor. The films connected with the uncertainty of Western society's collective psyche as 2000 approached. Anxieties were surfacing as they have tended to at the turn of previous centuries. On this occasion, film was a vehicle through which they could be made manifest. In a world where the future seems less certain than ever, the image of a meteor wreaking devastation expresses the deep-seated fear of what tomorrow might bring. It is a metaphor relating to fears about the fragility of human existence.

Life Beyond Death

The Oscar-laden Roman epic *Gladiator* (Ridley Scott, 2000) carried a strong theme of belief in the afterlife. The film begins and ends with a vision of the main character, Maximus (Russell Crowe), walking in the fields of Elysium—a place beyond death. At various points Maximus also prays to the gods and to his ancestors, the continuity between this life and the next being taken for granted.

The Sixth Sense (M Night Shyamalan, 1999) and *The Others* (Alejandro Amenábar, 2001) each explore the theme of what happens after death. Both films portray death not as an end but a point beyond which there is a different kind of life in which personality and individuality is not lost. They also have in common an excellent twist at the end of the story!

Identity and Self-Worth

In *American Beauty* (Sam Mendes, 1999) the underbelly of American middle-class suburbia is exposed. As already mentioned, many of the characters have lost sight of the things that really matter. Power, possessions and the quest for status in society are shown up for what they are as lives fall apart and spirits are crushed.

Bridget Jones' Diary (Sharon Maguire, 2001), a lighter film, touches some similar themes. Bridget (Renee Zellwegger) is driven by social expectations as much as by her own desires for a lasting relationship. It is as if she has no intrinsic identity and self-worth and is somehow dysfunctional because she has not found the right man.

An Open Invitation for a Christian Response

Christian faith must surely have something to say in response to the sort of issues raised in the above examples. In a world that is fearful for the future, Christian hope is a valuable commodity that needs to be shared. In a society that yearns to know that death is not the end, but for which it is a taboo subject, the good news of a God who has conquered the power of death needs to be heard. Where people are increasingly valued for what they do and what they have instead of who they are, their dignity as unique people created in the image of God needs to be affirmed.

Whether the film has supported or challenged a Christian view is secondary to the conversation possibilities that open up

The evangelistic challenge to the churches is to initiate conversation between the themes of film and the themes of faith. Importantly, the starting point is on the 'neutral ground' of a popular cultural phenomenon. The shared experience of having watched a particular film provides a ready-made opportunity for dialogue. Whether the film has supported or challenged a Christian view on the world is secondary to the conversation possibilities that open up. The potential is there irrespective of the film genre or its rating because films are, primarily, stories about people journeying through life and facing what comes their way.

There is also an 'arms-length' advantage in a faith and film encounter. Difficult questions and uncomfortable issues can be tackled initially through the safe distance of identifying with characters and situations on-screen—guilt and the need for forgiveness; the painful reality of broken relationships and the joy of restoration; despair and hope; fear or faith for the future, and the list goes on. These things are the very stuff of life and are not always easy for people to face. However, most people will have an opinion about the behaviour of a character that they have observed in a film. That opinion will often reflect something of the viewer's own outlook on life. Sometimes, it can be a short step from exploring responses to a film to exploring questions of personal faith.

Some Lessons from Experience 4

'Today a great many people, some within but many more without the church, find in a good film satisfaction and meaning similar to that once found in an essay, novel, poem, or sermon. Although film is mainly "just entertainment" for most people, for a growing number, both young and older adults, it provides food for thought, patterns for relating to others, values to strive for and assimilate, and mediated experiences of relating with unusual people in familiar and exotic settings.'

Edward McNulty, Presbyterian pastor[27]

One of the most exciting things about using film as a means of exploring questions of faith is its capacity to surprise—both yourself as the facilitator of the process and those taking part. In fact, if there is a rule of thumb, it is to expect the unexpected! This may seem a little daunting, but with a little forethought, sensitivity to the situation, and some flexibility in responding, the process is manageable. A few examples from my own experience may help.

The first involved an unstructured use of a film. It was an attempt to bring together a group of people from a socially deprived area, primarily to enjoy each other's company though hoping for an opportunity to connect the gospel with the film in a relevant way. The context was not one in which people generally attended such things as house groups or Bible studies. There were social and cultural reasons for this as well as a pervasive lack of self-esteem. Following eighteen months of struggle to bring people together, my wife and I unexpectedly found our living room packed with members of the local church and some of their friends. The opportunity to watch a film together was clearly a bigger draw than a conventional study group! I used the BBC film *Shadowlands* (Norman Stone, 1987), the portrayal of the love between C S Lewis (Joss Ackland) and Joy Davidman (Claire Bloom) for two reasons: it contained some fairly clear Christian themes; and it was reasonably short (89 minutes).

The opportunity to watch a film together was clearly a bigger draw than a conventional study group!

My hope was that discussion would happen spontaneously following the film over tea, coffee and bite to eat (though I did have a few discussion starters up my sleeve). As the film ended one of the oldest members in the group, a widow of three years following over fifty years of marriage, burst into tears. Initially this was a response to the film, but very quickly the woman spoke about the death of her husband *for the first time*. This in turn enabled a number of her friends to reach out to her in a way that had not been possible before. Her grief had been bottled up and the film enabled its release. It was late evening by the time people left, having shared with each other something of their own hopes and fears about life beyond this life.

It was a humbling experience and an opportunity to share the Christian hope of eternal life in a way that was relevant to the context and unforced. I anticipated that the film would raise questions about death but could not have envisaged the way in which people would minister to each other as a result of the evening.

The second example took place in a very different social context. Most people taking part were articulate professionals. My task was to facilitate a weekend preparation for Advent. The church concerned incorporated within its ministry a wide range of groups that met at various points during the week. Diverse beliefs were held in a creative tension and the make-up of those taking part in the weekend reflected this. My approach was to structure the weekend around a single film, showing it in three sections and setting up a range of ways for people to respond. The film used was *Awakenings* (Penny Marshall, 1990), based on the true story of a doctor working in a hospital in the Bronx for people with chronic mental illness during the late 1960s. (The actual film is, however, secondary to the process. Most films fall into fairly distinct sections and therefore lend themselves to being used over a number of sessions).

It was an opportunity to relate the gospel message in a context of openness rather than confrontation

I used the film as the starting point for people to consider both their own moments of 'awakening,' the times when they had glimpsed the transcendent and experienced a fullness of life, and also the things that diminish that sense of joy and wonder. The weekend included time for discussion, for worship together, and for people to make creative responses to what had been triggered in them by the film. It was an amazing time and some profoundly moving things were shared by those taking part with music, poetry, painting and sculpture emerging.

Bearing in mind the unconventional make-up of this group of around twenty people not all of the responses fell within the orthodox Christian camp! But in a climate of mutual respect and where all taking part were spiritual seekers, it was a real opportunity to relate the message of the gospel to the responses that the film evoked with honest and integrity in a context of openness rather than confrontation.

The third example is that of a workshop on faith and film run at a strong evangelical church. The group comprised around fifty people. The purpose of the particular workshop, the first of three, was to consider the power of film to engage the emotions and the subsequent need for the churches to be aware of this in order to respond appropriately. Part of the workshop involved some film clips to trigger different emotions in people, one of which was sadness. To do this, I used the section from *Four Weddings and Funeral* (Mike Newell, 1994) involving the death of one of the characters and the subsequent funeral service.

Film can strike chords within people in ways that cannot be foreseen

What happened next was not anticipated. One of the men became overcome with grief to the extent that it was necessary to stop the workshop for a short while to allow everyone a chance to recover. My assumption was that the man had recently been bereaved and that the film clip had touched a raw nerve. The reality, as I discovered later, was very different. The man was a leader in the church and had a close relative who had recently declared that he was gay. The character that died in the film was also gay and *that* was the point of emotional connection.

What I learnt on that occasion was how film can strike chords within people in ways that cannot always be foreseen. There is something risky about using film but it is manageable if sensitively handled. For the man in question, his minister was able to offer counsel and support. For the rest of those taking part, the events of the workshop simply accentuated the potential of film to touch the deepest places.

The fourth example is that of using one of the Jesus films. During a course exploring Christian basics as a 'refresher' for members of a particular church plus enquirers, in one session I used the crucifixion scene from *Jesus of Nazareth* (Franco Zefirelli, 1977). One of the participants had been a regular churchgoer for thirty years but that short section of film brought home to her, in a way that had never previously happened during her entire Christian journey, the extent of God's love. It knocked her for six for several weeks but reinvigorated her faith.

There is something risky about using film but it is manageable if sensitively handled

Having considered some specific experiences, I would now like to offer some general observations about using film in different ways. These represent a distillation of work relating faith and film in a variety of contexts over a number of years.

From a Structured Approach to an Open Agenda

It is possible to facilitate interaction with a film by carefully planning the process and providing a guiding framework. Equally, it is possible to simply provide an opportunity for people to respond to a film with the minimum of predetermined structure (generic examples of both are included in the next chapter).

The structured approach involves being clear about what is to be addressed. While it is always helpful to plan *some* space for unstructured responses to a film/film clips, this approach for responding to a film will have a particular aim and a method of achieving it.

Some Advantages of the Structured Approach

- Clarity and direction—people are able to get to grips with the subject in an ordered way.

- Themes and issues can be tackled deliberately and systematically— this makes it easy, for example, to plan a local church's study programme.

- A clear agenda—people understand the purpose of the use of a particular film/film clips from the outset.

Some Disadvantages of the Structured Approach

- There is a danger of stifling spontaneous responses to a film or film clips—not everyone would identify the same issues without some prompting.

- It is easy to undermine the integrity of a film by bending it too far in order to relate to the subject being tackled—like taking a text out of context simply to make a point.

An open agenda approach is a little riskier. Clearly, there still needs to be a purpose in mind for the session and a film will be chosen for a reason. For example, there could be a strong theme of hope running through a film and this could be a means of providing an opportunity for people to consider what Christian hope is all about. The difference is that the emphasis within the session is to allow the film to set the agenda.

Paradoxically, using film in this way is no less dependent upon a clear framework than is the structured approach. The difference is that the framework is far less prescriptive in terms of subject matter. For example, instead of inviting people to relate biblical passages identified beforehand to a declared theme within a film, a session might include space for people to make their own connections with whatever has emerged during the interaction with a film.

Some Advantages of the Open Agenda Approach

- Opportunity arises to be surprised by a film—it is not always the most obvious things that touch people most deeply.

- Freedom to respond to diverse issues that might be raised—of particular relevance in a postmodern culture.

Some Disadvantages of the Open Agenda Approach

- It is not always neat and tidy—while no less relevant to exploring faith than a structured approach.

- Unpredictability—it is not possible to anticipate every issue that might be generated by a film, some of which will generate controversy.

Not all faith and film encounters will involve either/or approaches. Often sessions will make use of the benefits of a structured *and* an open agenda approach. There is no reason why both a planned interaction with a specific theme as well as opportunity to respond to whatever a film evokes cannot be included in the same session. Such sessions often prove to be the most productive.

As one strand of a church's evangelistic strategy, faith and film sessions could be run as one-off events to which interested enquirers could be invited. Equally a series of sessions could be organized as part of a local church's ongoing programme of outreach. Whatever approach is adopted, the significance of film as a familiar cultural expression with which people are comfortable should not be underestimated. The common currency that film represents opens up an exciting range of opportunities, both to create points of contact for the gospel with non-Christians, and also to help those already within the church explore their faith further.

5 Getting Involved

'But rather than recounting the suspicion and fear that has sometimes prevailed in the church as it has considered the power of film in our lives, I need to tell the other side of the story as well. For movies have also proven to be a force for healing and insight. The power of film can change lives and communicate truth; it can reveal and redeem.'

Robert K Johnston[28]

There are plenty of opportunities for incorporating the use of film into the ongoing life and mission of the local church. For example, films could be used as a means of exploring Christian faith in relation to contemporary issues that are portrayed within them. They could be used to explore specific theological themes in depth. Or they could be used specifically for evangelistic purposes by utilizing them as a means of opening up a dialogue with the gospel message. The widespread availability of films on video cassette and DVD for rental or retail makes it an easily accessible resource. In particular, films on video are now very affordable.

With enough motivation, there is no real reason why even the smallest church could not begin to realize the potential of film as a vehicle for exploring faith. Of course, the demands of Christian leadership and pressures on time can often stifle innovation. For that reason I now offer a number of practical ideas and frameworks, along with a brief comment on available resources.

Preparing the Ground

It can be a real eye-opener for people to discover just how familiar they are with the medium of film. A good starting point is to develop some discussion and dialogue. Questions such as these work well in opening up conversation:

- 'What would your three favourite films of all time be, and why?
- 'If you could be one character from a film, who would it be and why?'
- 'Which film has had the most powerful impact upon you, and why?'

- 'Can you recall a film that has challenged, disturbed, or strengthened your faith in God in any way?'
- 'If you have seen any film portrayals of Jesus, how realistic do you think they were?'

There is seldom any difficulty in generating responses to such questions, and often groups will become very animated. One important reason for this is that there is almost always a shared knowledge about the films and characters that people mention. This common currency produces the basis for a good level of interaction between people regardless of how well they know each other.

Another possibility for generating thinking about film is to raise some questions and offer some comment on high-profile popular films. It is impossible for people to remain unaware of the films that stare out at us at bus stops, from roadside hoardings and in the media. Many people will have opinions about the films regardless of whether they actually see them.

Tapping into people's awareness and insights into film requires very little effort and is more about bringing what is already there to the surface rather than introducing something new and strange. Once this basic level of film awareness is achieved, the way is open for an encounter with film to be developed further. The possibilities are many. Here are three.

The Cinema Encounter

One of the most enjoyable ways of creating the opportunity for faith and film to be brought into conversation is to organize an evening out to the cinema. Minimal preparation is required apart from deciding which film and encouraging people to take part. Following the film, a brief and informal get-together over a coffee might be all that there is time for but even that will provide the opportunity to spark some thinking and reflection. A subsequent meeting, perhaps later in the week, could then enable the development of some more structured responses to the film.

Exploring a Specific Theme—A Structured Approach

It will sometimes be the case that a specific theme runs strongly through a film. Such films lend themselves to group activity and discussion. There are various publications now available containing developed responses to particular films (see below). The ideal use of a film is on the basis that everyone taking part in a group has already seen it. However, in a busy world that is not always possible. Consequently it is important to provide a concise summary of the film and set the scene for any clips of film used in a session.

As with many group sessions, an ice-breaker is helpful. It is then a good idea to introduce a film clip early on. Responses can be invited to the clip in relation to the theme that is being addressed. There is virtually no limit to the ways in which responses can be facilitated. Immediate reactions could be gathered in through a brainstorm exercise. People could be asked to identify with characters in the film and respond in role to set questions. Discussion could take place about ways in which the clip might inform or challenge people's perception of the theme that the session is seeking to address. Depending upon the group, opportunity could be provided for creative responses to be made (for example, paint, sculpture, writing).

With the theme identified beforehand, as well as inviting people to make their own links between the film clip and their own faith experience, it is also helpful to incorporate into the session some reference to relevant biblical passages. This helps maintain some cohesiveness in developing the theme that is addressed by the film.

If the film is being used in an evangelistic context it will be important to include space in the session for exploring issues such as:

- How the gospel message illuminates the relationships and situations portrayed in the film.

- Ways in which the film informs, supports or challenges the values of the kingdom of God.

- The nature of good news in relation to the aspects of the film—for example the implications for particular characters in the film if they were to embrace it.

These are challenging issues for anyone taking part in the session but the fact that the focus is on the film clip will often open the way for a real encounter with the gospel message to take place. Sometimes people who are reluctant to explore their own response to the gospel are enabled to do so through this type of 'one-step removed' approach. Very quickly, echoes are picked up between issues arising from a film or film clip and the reality of a person's own life. The gospel thus gets under the guard. That said, any use of a film for evangelistic purposes should always be declared as such from the outset.

The power of film to generate responses in people is such that a single film clip will often provide more than enough material to fuel a complete session. Several different clips can also be used to good effect in developing a theme, and they do not necessarily need to be from the same film.

An Open Approach to Using Film

When using a film in this way, the main difference to the specific theme approach is that the agenda is set by the film itself. Much of the structure of such a session will remain the same, but instead of formulating opportunities to respond in relation to an identified theme the challenge is to draw out and develop whatever emerges from the group. Clearly, in the context of using film within the Christian community, the intention is to engage Christian faith but the direction of a session is allowed to flow from whatever emerges from the film.

Some general questions that are useful in drawing out responses to a film/film clip within an open approach session (though by no means confined to the open approach) are:

- What, for you, was the most significant moment in the film and why?

- What are the positive things that you take away from what you have seen and why?

- In what ways are you challenged by the film?

- Which aspects of the film do you regard as being consistent with a Christian perspective on life, and where are the points of disagreement?

While an open approach is less predictable there is immediacy about the way in which people respond that provides a strong indicator of the nerves that are being touched by a film. This provides a very pertinent way of enabling Christian engagement with the statements, assumptions and portrayal of contemporary culture within a film. Once again, opportunities can be created to explore the relevance of the gospel message to questions raised.

The significance of popular film within contemporary culture can hardly be overstated. Life is permeated by its presence in a way that cries out for a Christian response. For the Christian community to turn its back on such an opportunity would be a tragedy, missing out on an unparalleled shared point of contact. With the resources now available and the motivation to make a start it would take very little to get a faith and film group off the ground. So if you have not yet used film as a means of evangelistic encounter, why not give it a go?

Some Practical Resources

Magazines

Empire and *Premiere*—each include reviews of new releases at the cinema and on video/DVD.

Sight and Sound—provides a helpful synopsis and critical analysis of all new releases.

Books

Some useful titles for getting started, all containing practical worked examples:

Reel Issues and *Reel Issues: The Sequel*, Ian Maher (Swindon: Bible Society, 1997 and 2001)

Praying the Movies: Daily Meditations from Classic Films, Edward McNulty (Louisville, Kentucky: Geneva Press, 2001)

Reflections on the Movies, Ken Gire (Colorado Springs: Victor, 2000)

For those looking to go deeper:

Reel Spirituality: Theology and Film in Dialogue, Robert K Johnston (Grand Rapids: Baker Academic, 2000)

Explorations in Theology and Film, Clive Marsh and Gaye Ortiz (eds) (Oxford: Blackwell, 1997)

Websites Worth a Look—A Few Examples

www.hollywoodjesus.com—'Visual movies reviews, with explorations into the deeper more profound meaning behind film, music and pop culture.' Over 61 *million* hits in four years.

www.damaris.org.uk—'Helps people relate Christian faith and contemporary culture.' Includes a range of current film reviews, accompanied by Christian comment and study material.

www.word-on-the-web.co.uk *(Maher at the Movies)*—A Church Army project that includes a monthly film review with some Christian reflection.

Using Film with Integrity

Some guidelines in the absence of any succinct statement defining the legal use of video.

- Using videos for private domestic viewing is perfectly legal.

- Education institutions are often copyright exempt and it may be that some church events could be classed as 'adult education.'[29]

- The Church Video Licence scheme provides legal coverage for using an increasing range of videos in the context of church activities. Further details are available from: Christian Video Licensing Europe Ltd, Chantry House, 22 Upperton Road, Eastbourne BN21 1BF. Tel: 01323–417711. Email: info@ccli.co.uk. Website: www.ccli.co.uk.

- Filmbank Distributors Ltd provides videos licensed for public use. They are more expensive but of higher quality than retail outlet videos. Further details from: Filmbank Distributors Ltd, 98 Theobald's Road, London WC1X 8WB. Tel: 020–7984–5966. Website: www.filmbank.co.uk.

In addition, Roger Standing's observation is a good one for any church to bear in mind: 'The copyright law is there to protect the artists, filmmakers and production companies. Many churches therefore endeavour to purchase a copy of any video they use so that the appropriate amount of money goes to the appropriate places. As the video clips can have a promotional value for the product, this may offer a workable way forward, with integrity.'[30]

Notes

1 Kevin Spacey won an Oscar for his performance as Lester Burnham in this 1999 film by British Director Sam Mendes.

2 Ken Gire, *Reflections on the Movies* (Colorado Springs: Victor, 2000) p 39.

3 Cited in Robert G Konzelman, *Marquee Ministry: The Movie Theater as Church and Community Forum* (New York: Harper and Row, 1971) p 13.

4 See *British Film Institute Film and Television Handbook 2001* (London: BFI).

5 2 Samuel 12.1–7.

6 Ken Gire, *Reflections on the Movies* (Colorado Springs: Victor, 2000) p 11.

7 T S Eliot, 'Religion and Literature' in *Essays Ancient and Modern* (New York: Harcourt, Brace and World, 1936); rpt in *The New Orpheus: Essays toward a Christian Poetic*, N A Scott, Jr (ed) (New York: Sheed and Ward, 1964) p 227.

8 Ian Maher, *Reel Issues* (Swindon: Bible Society, 1998) pp 3-5.

9 Roger Angell, 'Mean Streets' in *The New Yorker*, February 18, 1980, p 128.

10 John R May, *Image and Likeness: Religious Visions in American Film Classics* (New Jersey: Paulist Press, 1992) p 3.

11 Sources: British Film Institute website (www.bfi.org.uk), August 2001.

12 That is, non-magical people (in case you have yet to be 'Pottered'). For engaging with some of issues arising from the Harry Potter phenomenon, see Philip Plyming's, *Harry Potter and the Meaning of Life* (Grove Spirituality booklet S 79).

13 *The Independent*, 28 December 1998.

14 *The Times*, 4 June 1999.

15 For example, the conclusions of the 1997 Home Office study differed from a report entitled *Violence, Pornography and the Media* that was submitted to the Parliamentary All Party Family and Child Protection Group in June of the previous year.

16 *The Independent*, 29 December 1997.

17 *The Independent*, 24 July 1999.

18 William Peter Blatty, *The Exorcist* (London: Blond and Briggs, 1972) .

19 C Marsh and G Ortiz, *Explorations in Theology and Film* (Oxford: Blackwell, 1997) ch 2.

20 Cited on the flyleaf in Gaye Ortiz and Clive Marsh, *Explorations in Theology and Film* (Oxford: Blackwell, 1997)

21 Ken Gire, *Reflections on the Movies* (Colorado Springs: Victor, 2000) p 39.

22 C S Lewis, *An Experiment in Criticism* (London: Cambridge University Press, 1961) p 19, cited by Ken Gire *op cit.*

23 Robert McKee, *Story* (New York: Harper Collins Publishers, 1997) p 25

24 Robert K Johnston, *Reel Spirituality* (Grand Rapids: Baker Academic, 2000) pp 25–26.

25 For some more detailed practical tips, see Ian Maher, *Reel Issues* (Swindon: Bible Society, 1998) pp 4–10.

26 Film reviews are widely available in printed form and on the Internet. Some examples are cited at the end of this booklet.

27 Edward McNulty, *Praying the Movies* (Louisville, Kentucky: Geneva Press, 2001) p xii.

28 Robert K Johnston, *Reel Spirituality* (Grand Rapids: Baker Academic, 2000) p 24.

29 Roger Standing, *Preaching for the Unchurched*, (Grove Evangelism booklet Ev 58) pp 26–7.

30 *ibid*, p 27.